Caleb the Campervan Visits Europe

CALEB AND THE FERRY

by
DONNA LODGE

Caleb the campervan visits Europe © Copyright <<2023>> Donna Lodge

All rights reserved. No part of this publication may be reproduced, distributed or transmitted in any form or by any means, including photocopying, recording, or other electronic or mechanical methods, without the prior written permission of the publisher, except in the case of brief quotations embodied in critical reviews and certain other noncommercial uses permitted by copyright law.

Although the author and publisher have made every effort to ensure that the information in this book was correct at press time, the author and publisher do not assume and hereby disclaim any liability to any party for any loss, damage, or disruption caused by errors or omissions, whether such errors or omissions result from negligence, accident, or any other cause.

Adherence to all applicable laws and regulations, including international, federal, state and local governing professional licensing, business practices, advertising, and all other aspects of doing business in the US, Canada or any other jurisdiction is the sole responsibility of the reader and consumer.

Neither the author nor the publisher assumes any responsibility or liability whatsoever on behalf of the consumer or reader of this material. Any perceived slight of any individual or organization is purely unintentional.

The resources in this book are provided for informational purposes only and should not be used to replace the specialized training and professional judgment of a health care or mental health care professional.

Neither the author nor the publisher can be held responsible for the use of the information provided within this book. Please always consult a trained professional before making any decision regarding treatment of yourself or others.

ISBN: 979-8-89109-543-4 - paperback
ISBN: 979-8-89109-544-1 - ebook

CALEB THE CAMPERVAN SONG

Caleb the campervan is coming out today.
Caleb the campervan is coming out to play.
Momma and Pompsy hop inside.
Where will they go today for a ride?

If you want to receive the musical score
for this and hear the song being sung,
please visit the following website:
www.donnalodge.com

Caleb rocked with excitement. He was going on a tour around Europe with Momma and Pompsy. He looked forward to visiting new countries, learning new languages, and travelling on a ferry.

Momma and Pompsy beamed as they picked up their translation books. Their first stop was France. 'Au revoir!' Momma and Pompsy giggled as they waved goodbye to their family.

As they approached the ferry port, Caleb saw lots of other vehicles, including cars, lorries, and campervans.

Pompsy waved to all the VW campervan drivers.
Momma waved at every campervan.
She always mixed up the vans!

All the lorries were loaded onto the deck. Caleb's tummy flip-flopped with joy as he dreamed of an adventure with his favourite humans.

Caleb was surprised, though, when Momma and Pompsy jumped out of the van and started to walk towards the human's deck. Caleb started to feel scared. He didn't want to be left on the vehicle deck on his own. Momma spotted his sad face and shouted, 'Don't worry, Caleb! We'll be back soon.'

The floor started to move as the boat left the port. The vehicle deck went dark. Caleb suddenly felt sick. He let out a sob. 'I don't like it!' he cried.

'Hey, little fellow. Don't be afraid,' said the lorry next to him. 'My name is Laurence, and I'm French, but you English vehicles call me Larry Lorry.

There's nothing to be afraid of. I do this trip twice each week. The humans always come back for us! Any minute now, the car deck party will start.'

Just as Larry said this, some of the other lorries started chanting. 'Let's all play! The adults are away!'

Larry winked at Caleb and honked his horn loudly.
Other cars started sounding their car alarms.
Even Caleb joined in the fun by flashing his lights.

'Now it's time for the vehicle shuffle!' shouted a big motorhome at the front of the queue. 'You'll love this,' said Larry. 'This is when the disco begins.'

'Follow my moves, and keep up with everyone,' Larry said as the motorhome at the front started to chant the words to the vehicle shuffle.

'Turn your wheels to the right. Yeeha!
Turn your wheels to the left. Oh, yeah!

Shimmy forward. Woohoo!
Shake it out. Shake! Shake!'

In no time at all, Caleb knew the moves to the vehicle shuffle. He danced along with all the other vehicles. He had never had such fun!

'Quiet! We're near the port!' shouted a lorry as the deck lights came on. Larry winked at Caleb. 'This is a vehicle secret,' he told him. 'We don't let the humans know about our parties.' All the vehicles pretended to be calmly waiting for their owners to return.

'Here we are, Caleb,' said Momma.
'I hope you haven't been too lonely.'
Pompsy couldn't understand why
Caleb's windscreen wipers were swishing and
his lights were on. He felt sure he had turned
them off before he'd left Caleb on the car deck.

As Caleb waited to leave the ferry, Larry told him, 'You'll love France. You'll learn to count in French! Un, deux, trois!' Larry waved as he left the ferry.

Caleb flashed his lights to thank Larry for being such a good friend and looking after him.

In France, Momma and Pompsy smiled. They shouted 'Bonjour' or 'Hello' to everyone they saw.

Caleb had to drive on the opposite side of the road. Momma and Pompsy had to pay to use the roads by stopping at les péages.

It was such fun and so different from home. Vineyards grew all around, and Pompsy explained that the grapes were used to make wine.
'I'd love a glass of wine,' said Momma.

I love my European trip, he thought.
But after all that dancing, I need a rest.
'I don't know why Caleb is so tired today,'
said Pompsy. But we do, don't we?

Author Biography

Donna Lodge is a Mum, Grandma and Aunty with over 30 years teaching experience under her belt. She enjoys writing and the Caleb the Campervan series has emerged from her own experiences of travelling around Europe in a campervan and re-telling stories to her granddaughters, Isla and Isabelle.

www.ingramcontent.com/pod-product-compliance
Lightning Source LLC
Chambersburg PA
CBHW041412010526
44107CB00015B/1143